POTENT QUOTES
FOR SOUL

Uplifting
Quotes
For
Modern Life

Also other books by Eric Chifunda:

* Selected Inspirational Quotes

* An Endless Quest for Spiritual Truth:
a practical guide to everyday spirituality.

POTENT QUOTES FOR SOUL

Uplifting
Quotes
For
Modern Life

Eric Chifunda

ReadersMagnet, LLC

Contents

ACKNOWLEDGEMENT

I WANT TO EXPRESS MY heartfelt, profound eternal gratitude to my teacher, friend, Harold Klemp, who continually inspires me beyond words.

A word of thankful gratitude goes to Michele Bluestone (Bluestone Writing Group, LLC) who edited the book with professionalism, efficiency, care, and flexibility.

INTRODUCTION

ARE YOU LOOKING FOR A fresher and higher perspective in which to live your life? The answer may be in this book – Potent Quotes for Soul. Words of wisdom, from various guardian angels who act as spiritual guides (modern and ancient), may enlighten the reader, resulting in an attitude upliftment. With this positive difference in attitude can come a positive change in life. You can't continue with the same approach that brought and kept you where you are today and expect to get new results. An upgrade in one's attitude can be facilitated by reading the uplifting words written in this book. It is possible to gain the power to shape one's future to a more favorable outcome.

The words we read, our habitual thoughts, our tightly held beliefs can influence our attitudes. This change can significantly affect how we view our lives, and consequently, how we also live our lives. Thus the more uplifting the words, the higher they can elevate our attitude. And this can potentially help us live a more uplifting life, which can lead to the fulfillment of our destiny.

It helps to remember that we are all capable of being better than what we are today. And that journey toward developing a better version of ourselves can be ignited by reading these uplifting words that resonate with you that are in this book.

CHAPTER 1

THE JOURNEY

When God enters your life such that it permeates all your actions, It begins to work miracles in a way that makes your life a little more forgiving, smoother, and joyful that help improve your quality of life.

Often people have great ideas but lack the courage to bring them out, let alone act on them.

To survive in this world, you need to apply laws and rules of the land while remaining truthful in all you do.

To learn to love God in new ways requires an attitude of surrender, an open heart to love, patience, and courage to try new things.

You can't be fearful, passive, and expect to follow God fully. Life rewards the courageous: They are the true followers of God's uncompromising truth and guidance.

You can't limit Divine Spirit where it is meant to be fully expressed for too long without suffering the ill effects of such suppression.

When God is invited in what you do, there's no limit as to what resources you can draw on. The only limit is your own personal view that you impose upon yourself and the situation.

If you walk these turbulent grounds on Earth, while you maintain a high state of being, you are in heaven with God.

The trust you have in God is what keeps you firmly connected to God. When this connection is strong, only good can come out of you. This connection will carry you through good times, so you don't get too attached, thereby avoid being trapped by the allures of materiality. This connection will carry you through tough times which otherwise would crush you if you didn't have the strong connection.

The state of untruthfulness is a state of darkness in which you feel spiritually powerless, helpless, and lost. On the other hand, the state of truthfulness is a state of love, joy, freedom, and spiritual power. If you are firmly anchored in truth, you will get aligned with Divine Spirit at a deeper level which can help you meet your daily challenges with wisdom, aiding you in making right choices and consequently right actions.

Soul survives the pressures, the travails, the rigors of this world by remembering Its true nature. Its true nature is that of being indestructible. Once Soul recognizes this, there's no death as perceived at the human level. There's only translation from one state to another.

With Divine armor, you shall never be defeated. Victory will be yours. Victory in the ascendance into the heart of God whence ultimate survival is fulfilled to its utmost.

Past failures should never be overlooked for they serve as teaching tools to improve on future conditions.

By being clear channels, we allow God to take root in our consciousness. So stay clear, let the spirit of God come through; consequently, courage, strength, wisdom, and more importantly, love shall be the weapons you will possess to meet the challenges the world throws at you.

God's ways are many and always unique to each individual. You must find out what yours are. It's not always easy to do as the mind often stands in the way. This is so because the mind has always been in charge in this outer world. Yet, time and again, lovers of God have always found ways to outmaneuver the dominance of the mind and its base influence.

L et God be the source from which you draw your strength, courage, and inspiration to serve others.

God's plan for you, which inevitably comes with obstacles, is to learn to overcome these obstacles, which compel you to remain spiritually alert and aware of your own indestructible divine nature. It helps to remember that you, as Soul, can never be permanently defeated or crushed by any obstacles thrown at you. When you live as God intended for you, it means you acknowledge these obstacles as part of God's plan to help continually strengthen you spiritually for your survival and continual growth.

L oving God is never easy, yet it is doable if you learn how to trust, listen to God, and follow through with right action where necessary and as needed.

Love God so that you can become a co-worker in your own way, at your own level of consciousness, and with what you possess: your skills, talents, knowledge, and wisdom.

You are not to be a doormat, but verily a warrior who stands on his own feet and acts fairly to all, yet firmly when need arises. To succeed in this world and the next inner world, you need strength, courage, and above all love for truth, justice, and fairness.

Approach life as a contract to fulfill certain obligations. And strive to fulfill them diligently. Fulfilling the myriad of contracts brings about a positive personal transformation characterized by personal integrity, personal growth, and respect for people you deal and work with.

What good is being able to listen to God's voice without having the self-discipline, courage, and strength to act upon it? You can listen all you want, but if you don't follow through with what God wills you to do, what good is it?

Always look to God for perfect guidance as to whom to give love and when best to do it.

If truth is what you seek, no matter what happens to you, you will rise in truth to the very pinnacle of what is real and truthful.

Whenever you feel you are beginning to need somebody whereby you feel you can't do without the person, that is a sign that you may be inadvertently pushing the person away to the proportion that you excessively need them in an overly dependent way.

The law of love requires that we give to life what belongs to life. If you give to life honesty, you will get honesty back in some way in proportion to what and how much you have given.

Think about what is in your life and what you have neglected to take care of and move to attend to them promptly. For in life, you are always warned ahead of time before tragedy befalls you.

Act promptly and re-organize your life such that all necessary things you need to attend to are taken care of. For laws of life require that we conduct lives to reflect order, honesty, integrity, and love.

The laws of Divine Spirit are many, subtle, yet interconnected. To understand and know what they are, ask to be shown.

Mastering one's life entails maintaining the right attitude toward all you do and all who you meet. This attitude can best be described as a non-attached attitude. It is an attitude that lets all your actions, thoughts, and feelings flow freely, unencumbered by fear, undue attachment, greed, vanity, lust, and anger. When these Passions of the mind are brought under control, your actions are rendered pure and carry greater power, potency, and more effective than before.

To master your life, master how you give up all you do into the hands of God, so that God's hands become your hands.

Thoughtless acts oftentimes result in infraction of spiritual laws that in turn limit the flow of Divine Love.

Listen to God so you know what to do with your life, and eliminate unnecessary experiences that only serve to delay you, cause unwarranted hardships, and inconveniences. When God speaks, listen up, and take action with full trust that all will go well in the end.

Loving life means enjoying and partaking of it. You don't stand by the sideline and expect to enjoy life.

Life presents you with opportunities to take advantage of or if you delay, you are liable to lose them.

The key to good timing lies in listening to the inner voice of God to be guided as to when is the best time to take action.

To enjoy your life, go with what arises as spontaneous–at the moment. Don't wait for some expected right time. What is the right time for Divine Spirit, may not be what you wish it to be at the time the opportunity presents itself.

What you give is what you get back. It's the law of love, the law of life, and the law of nature that if we give something out, it must, by virtue of the law of action, respond at some point, now or later, in the like manner, though the outer appearance of it might be different.

Think about life as a classroom in which you learn basic principles which you apply to things, so we improve our chances of success. Success may either be characterized as having something positive come out of our effort in the immediate now, or our action get invested for future dividend or a bad situation gets resolved such that it is rendered unnecessary to happen again.

Life, as it is, is supposed to have deeper meaning and purpose for it to be of any worth. God did not give us life to be squandered. God gave us life, so something purposeful and spiritually significant can come of it.

Many times, as we go on with our daily lives, we lose focus and sight of our purpose on Earth. This loss of sight puts us at the mercy of the vagaries of life.

For life to have a higher purpose and deeper meaning, you must give back in some constructive way to serve life. In so doing, you will not only be helping yourself move forward, you will be helping others experience love, joy, and beauty as you become a source from which they get inspired to live a better life.

The end of ideas and plans should be action. Without action, you can do all the thinking and planning you want, conjure up great ideas, but without follow up action to crystallize these ideas into reality, they would be of no practical significance. So thinking outside the box not only helps move society forward through new inventions and new technologies but also it may help break up outmoded traditions which no longer serve any useful purpose in life.

Listen to God so you can know what needs to be done now to enable you to plan better for tomorrow. Your future depends on what you do today. Treat others well, and you will have sewn seeds that will return proportionate respect and good treatment from others. Remember when you treat others well, life will rearrange itself to serve you well.

Everyday should be another day to walk closer to God. Since each day should bring you closer to God, it means you will encounter new situations and conditions that often will be stepping stones to climb the spiritual ladder to the next rung–toward God.

Be patient whenever a new situation presents itself, for it could be God calling you to move closer to It. Be alert to the inner guidance, so you can get proper direction when in doubt.

One way to keep your heart open is by finding out what you love to do and doing it. In doing it, your life will turn around for the better. So look to God to be shown what you need to do in the moment and with your life if you already don't know or you are in doubt.

Oftentimes in life you will meet setbacks, obstacles, and discouragements, but don't let these hold you back. You are far greater than these obstacles of the negative force. They are forces of the negative power because their purpose is to stop you in your tracks so you don't fulfill God's dream for you.

Fear has the power to paralyze a person. This paralysis can stop one from making any effort to go beyond the familiar ground on which one stands. Such a person who is trapped by fear never gets to enjoy life because of unnecessary self-imposed restrictions which can keep one trapped within a certain limited aspect of the individual's life.

One with love who has learned through taking life by its horns, has the valor, the inherent adventuresome spirit alive in one, will always be willing to extend oneself to new territories. And always ready to serve others through one's abilities, talents, interests, and willingness to sacrifice for others without conditions.

Once we want something for ourselves at a personal and self-centered level, we often are imposing limiting conditions on a situation. But when we want something for the good of all, for universal good, then a transformation, in the sense of what we want, takes place. Suddenly what initially may have been a mundane and or a materialistic-driven want becomes a transcendent spiritual want. This type of want is often liberating, and it is not impeded in its manifestation by human interference.

Loving life at a deeper level entails surrendering your personal self-interest into the hands of God. When this happens, you will be making God come through to be an integral part of your experience. God may rearrange your life so that there's more enjoyment in your life.

Look to God to take care of all your affairs, be it work, school, social, health. Let God be in charge, but stay fully engaged in your daily activities while your inner state remains in a state of surrender to God.

CHAPTER 2

AWAKENING

The deeper you go in your realization of what you are as Soul, the more courage, inner strength, joy, and love for life you gain.

In letting God be number one in your life and all you do, you in turn become your best version, in your own way and to the best of your ability.

With right actions, the flow of Divine Spirit comes through. Without this outflow through right actions, It remains bottled in. Sooner or later you begin to feel stifled and stagnated in your consciousness. To go beyond this stagnation, we need to create an opening through loving actions in such a way that they serve a useful, higher purpose.

When you give of yourself to life, life embraces you in return. This increases the flow of Divine Spirit, leading to increased vibrancy in your spiritual awareness. The spiritualization of your inner state sensitizes your spiritual senses, making you a far-seeing individual. With great foresight, you are able to meet life a little more prepared.

When fears go, nothing can stop you from immersing yourself in life. Nothing can stop you from serving life.

Listen to God so that you can get directed to Its home by riding the love waves homeward through Sounds of God. These heavenly sounds serve one principal purpose, and that is to lift and free you from the bondages imposed upon you by yourself and society.

In letting go of your old self, you will be inviting the new self. This must be done through a process of purification, awakening, and right experiences that make you face yourself. You either conquer your outmoded old self as it continually manifests in your outer life or it conquers you.

The very fact that one has purity, gives one perception and clarity of sight, which those impure in thought and manner do not and can't possess.

The advantage of living a life of spirituality is that you maximize your blessings. You hear God more clearly; you see God more clearly; you want God more desperately than before; you want to share God more liberally and willingly than before; you become a more conscious child of God; you walk with God daily; and you want others to experience God like you have. You bring peace and hope in others' hearts and minds; you inspire others to find their own spiritual connection.

It's in surrender that God brings new changes in your life. It's in surrender that you open yourself to a higher reality. It's in surrender that you receive divine intervention. Without surrender, you remain trapped in your limited world of mind desires. So let go of your concerns, your negativity, and let God flush them out of your system so that your consciousness can be raised to a new level of awareness.

Truth as we know it is always clothed in something more acceptable. But often times we mistake the outer clothing for its substance that is often hidden behind its outer cover. Thus our search for truth often stops at the outer cover–we make a judgment; as a result, we stop there. Once we make a judgment about the appearance–the clothing–the substance of its inner truth is lost. We never get to the core of truth about the person or situation.

When you live your life as God intended for you, everything about your life expands and moves forward.

Listen to the inner voice of God constantly, and your life will be attuned constantly to that which is carved by the divine hand of God.

It takes total commitment to let God be your primary guide in your life. It takes purity of thought and consciousness to let Divine Spirit operate through you. It's in this state of purity that Divine Spirit manifests Itself and becomes an integral part of your outer reality.

ith higher awareness comes need for
high accountability.

When you seek God's guidance on a daily basis, your entire life gets transformed. You no longer do things that are superficial as your main core of your lifestyle without being aware in a relatively short time. Your senses get more acute in detecting entrapments, the negative force's cunning maneuvers. Your heart opens to let love come in and go out more appropriately.

Happiness can be cultivated in us and shared with others. Bear in mind that it is most felt and enjoyed once shared with those we love. It is in sharing that we become spiritually more alive.

Don't let anything happen to you unless, in some way, you allow it. So be careful; this is a cunning world where the negative force may come through the very people you consider as friends that may lead you in the direction you didn't plan to go—the wrong direction.

Higher truth can never be found in anything until your level of perception and acceptance expands.

People who are creative in certain areas are so because they are engaged in an activity that opens them up to their innermost part of themselves—the presence of God in them—which we all have. From this vantage point, they are able to come up with novel ideas emanating from a higher source within.

Despite limiting conditions we sometimes find ourselves in, life continually presents us with limitless opportunities to rise above them, designed to make us grow in our capacity for more love, therefore, yield a better quality of life and a heightened sense of wellbeing.

We are by nature, in the human state, beings subject to conditioning. Conditioning makes life easier as it takes less effort to go through routines than start new paths that require vigilance, risk-taking, and measurable discomfort, at times. Yet all progress entails change, risk, and it comes about by breaking the old routine in order to set us off on a new course.

Should you awaken your consciousness and withdraw from life, you are bound to have a backflow of this energy you have gained. It will leave you feeling overloaded, and you will overfill with it. Sooner or later, you will experience stagnation because you are not expending this love energy to build and to distribute it appropriately to achieve some end.

What makes one learn about the mysteries of God is an attitude driven by genuine desire to learn. This draws you out of your shell of self-imprisonment. You will never easily grow if you don't have a curious attitude. So always look to sharpen your spiritual senses so God can be yours to see in all things around you.

Dig deeply within your inner recesses of your heart to open yourself to an outpouring of new ideas that lurk hidden behind the conditioned human consciousness. Thinking outside the box means listening and trusting your inner higher part of yourself as a source of creative ideas that bring about a positive change to you and society at large.

Each situation will teach us a new lesson about how to love God a little more. This means growing in awareness of what and who God is.

To learn to love God in new ways requires an attitude of surrender, an open heart to love, patience, and courage to try new things.

The advantage of living an awakened life of spirituality is that you maximize your blessings. You hear God more clearly than before. You see God as Light more clearly. You feel God more strongly than before. You want God more desperately than before. You want to share God with others more liberally but discretely than before.

CHAPTER 3

SELF DISCOVERY

The sharpening of the mind makes the mind more complex yet quicker in its functioning as the intellectual baggage is cleansed by experiences in the Light and Sound of God.

When all actions are done with God in mind, then all you do becomes God-infused whether you are aware of it or not. These types of actions continually and steadily render you progressively, spiritually more alive.

Don't let the force of habit or fear dictate what you do if you aspire to live in the moment. Sometimes tough decisions are made when we are faced with an opportunity to do something we are not used to doing. So try to be courageous and embrace life fully and live it well.

Dedicate your life to finding truth, to recognize the truth, and the truth will be yours. What will happen is that you will touch the cloth of God at that moment when you find the truth. You will awaken a part of you, which was before not realized. Each time you discover the truth, you are actually discovering yourself.

Once the heart is rendered pure through spiritual training, one begins to see aspects of God within oneself, in others, and in life as it unfolds before one. One realizes that one is truly a *Divine Spark of God* that is indestructible, that has latent great awareness imbued with divine love.

The power of God is for those who have given up their personal wills. And in its place, they have accepted only Divine Will as their will. Yet to do so is to lose oneself and one's identity. But yet it's a spiritual requirement that you do so. You do so to let God's will override your will. It is this override that makes God manifest Itself in what you do.

What must you do to overcome the old obstacles that have become set in your life? You can start by looking at obstacles as opportunities for further advancement. Look at life as a gift to be lived and enjoyed.

Seek truth for the sake of it, and truth will always protect you. Remember that your idea of truth may not be others' idea of truth.

Learn to find truth in all you do, and the truth will be revealed to you. To do so, you must give up your preconceived notion of what truth might be. You will never know for sure what truth is till you find it. When you do, you will be surprised at its simplicity. You will be happy with its liberating effect.

When you follow God wherever It takes you, you will find yourself doing things, which at times, defy logic. You will find yourself trusting a power greater than intellect. You will find yourself climbing spiritual mountains, which before seemed insurmountable. You will find yourself turning negative situations into positive ones. You will find yourself controlling situations instead of them controlling you. You will find yourself in charge–in the driver's seat, instead of life dragging you along. You will find yourself pulling life along to catch up with you instead of you playing catch up.

You are a true warrior when you start scaling the heights of the heavens while here on Earth. The strength you gain from these inner travels should be applied to enable you to survive the rigors of this physical world.

Soul gives its pure love in a state of freedom. So, create a condition whereby the other Soul can express freedom without conditions imposed on them.

Divine Spirit has a way of showing you how to find truth in the most unlikely and unexpected ways and places. Sometimes where you think you might find truth, it may never be there. Truth is not always clothed in something that fits our expectation of it.

Each time you discover truth, you are actually discovering yourself. For what is truth other than you looking back at yourself; for you only see in life that which relates to you in your consciousness.

If you seek mundane experiences and outer realty and accept its reality, for you, the mundane will be real and spirituality unreal. If you seek and love the spiritual reality and have your inner existence in that state, your world will be lifted to new horizons.

To love truth for the sake of it, you must seek it without prejudgment. You must be willing to accept truth on its own terms.

It's your mission to discover truth. It's your birthright to awaken to higher truth and cherish it. Keep in mind that to sincerely love truth is the initial step to finding it.

A God lover knows his mission. A God lover knows where he stands in life. A God lover has power to help others in unselfish way. A God lover is a trusted friend. A God lover is patient. A God lover strives for excellence and does the best he can.

Your natural true interests are actually God interests that God has instilled in you. So by engaging in them, you are in truth engaging God.

We are spiritual beings; therefore, everything we do, though they may appear mundane, must be based in basic good conduct of honesty.

One needs to choose between being a doormat or someone who stands up for what is right and respectful. So look at your life and see where you have neglected to right the wrong that was perpetrated against you by some uncaring, thoughtless, and or disrespectful individual. Use that as a teaching tool to adjust your own attitude to enable you to meet your next challenges in order to thwart the reoccurrence of the same.

I f you love God in the usual way you have always done, you may limit yourself from loving God more. Keep in mind that you have to learn to love God more in new ways like you never did before in order to continue to grow in your capacity for more love.

God gives us gifts to be passed on by us to the world. And we must obey this mandate from God. Failure to do so leaves us evermore unfulfilled. Find ways and people that support your dream, and you will make your life more abundant spiritually, and you may become materially self-sufficient.

Divine love has the power to break the very personal shackles that hold you in bondage to this world of phenomenon. Your world of phenomenon is a world devoid of the true light of God. It's a world of darkness whence real truth has diminished existence.

To live a life of freedom, in the presence of light, you must always not concern yourself too much with various outer aspects of life activities, but more so with the flow of Divine Spirit to Its source, where everything comes in synch with one another. Then you can live in freedom, in the light, and not in darkness.

Soul, as it is tested through challenges, falling and getting back up, progressively matures and begins to realize Its true nature. It gets purified, and once this happens, It learns how to live life more lovingly. It learns to meet life challenges more adeptly. It learns to approach life more spiritually. It learns to depend on God for Its guidance for all It does.

Love can never be pretended for long. Love is real; hence you can never fake it for too long. If you fake it, sooner or later, it will uncover the fake veneer, thus expose a lie that may exist behind the façade of fake love.

God created humans and implanted gifts in them, which as they unfold and get ready at a particular time in one of their incarnations, one is able to recognize what they are. Once one recognizes what these gifts are, the next task for one is to find ways to make them a reality. Making these a reality is part of honoring the contract one has with Divine Spirit.

Your responsibility is to identify your gifts, capitalize on them, and pass them to the world. Why pass them? Because they belong there. They are not meant for you to keep, but to be shared with the world, so that the world can be enriched by your actions.

God does not seek recognition for all the miracles that issue from It. You, too, being God's child, should not seek recognition lest you fall from the spiritual pedestal.

Remember, God's home encompasses all universes. Your home as God's child should, therefore, encompass all universes. If you learn the secret of being a citizen of the universes, you will become a universal man indeed.

The invisible world is a real world in which those who gain mastery over their lives are able to access it. They give up the lower world so that the inner becomes their world from which they view life. It becomes a world in which they have their conscious existence. This is crucial to living a full life.

CHAPTER 4

HIGHER LOVE

When Soul sees that the love from another Soul is unconditional, It draws closer to that Soul. But once conditions are placed, they become barriers that keep Souls asunder.

Give love such that it is never imposing but allows the other person their space and freedom to love you in their own way. You have love in your heart, and you are free to express it in your own way and so do others.

A God lover never shies away from doing God's work. A God lover recognizes his role, his mission in life, to express love and help lead others to find God in this lifetime.

It's by connecting with others through loving actions do we serve God well. So, keep good conduct of respectfulness and love, so God can find you good grounds upon which to share love with others.

With love as your daily gift to life, you will live in God's presence at all times.

Matters of the heart can never be reduced to the analysis of the mind. Matters of pure love do not issue from the mind, but truly from the pure essence of God. To understand this pure love, you ought to let go of the mind and its analysis. Through analysis, the power of love dims and slips away.

Life without love is empty even if it may appear laden with materiality. Life with love is fulfilling and rich even though one may have few material things to show for it. Richness lies in the abundance of love you possess and give out to the world.

When a woman loves a man, it can be the beginning of the man's journey to his innermost love center if she knows how to love him without possessing him. Her love for her man would soften his ego so that his higher Soul self would shine through. Ego blinds man to his higher divine self.

When love is true and fully given by the woman to her man, the man's center of love is stimulated. This stimulation allows love to come forth from his heart to hers. The outflow of love from a woman leaves her enriched, liberated.

Accumulate spiritual wealth by investing in love in your life. Love invested now becomes a future blessing.

When you have love in your heart, in your life, in all you do, and that is the basis for your actions, you will live this life in the light and not in the dark.

God's love is best expressed through work done diligently and done well. Diligent work entails attention to details. It demands high standards of performance and an open heart that gives it its all.

What good is love if it cannot be shared with others? It's in sharing that we greatly appreciate its value. It is in appreciation that we grow in our capacity to love more. It's in loving more that we understand our divinity. It is in our divinity that we have Divine Love. With divine love, we live in the presence of God.

It is in loving truth that you find its hidden yet simple ways. Small acts of kindness, fairness, and respect for others yield feelings of love that connect you with those you give these gifts of Divine Spirit. Once you breathe the essence of God into all you do, God will in turn embrace you in Its protective arms.

Love can never stay locked in the heart and have the same effect. It's in its action that it is of any value to you and the recipient. So to be enriched with love; you must appropriately give it out as much as you possibly can.

One who has a greater awareness of truth has a greater capacity for love. But the value of love can only be appreciated by what we do with it and not how we hold it in.

God's love is unselfish, unlimited, and always aims at opening people's hearts through the connection they make with other people.

To have love come into your life, firstly learn how to appropriately give it. Then stay open to receiving the return flow of love that comes back your way. You must do something with this return flow of love—share it.

Give love to those who need it, but do it in such a way that it serves a need in their life.

To find love you must look for it in the right places. You can find it if you start to genuinely seek it. Sincerity in your desire to find love is the first step.

Attempts to possess another are often futile and puts another in an uncomfortable position. So free yourself from possessive love. Learn to love freely.

When you love God with all your heart, you are, in effect, giving your life to God, which in turn gives it back to you a hundredfold. So to get your life to become enriched, surrender your health, anxieties, fears, and possessions into the loving arms of God. It will in turn shape, protect, heal, and re-organize your life to reflect Its miraculous master hand at work.

If you learn how to think in terms of how what you do will benefit others, you will find that your actions will become selfless, expansive, and more productive.

When you act out of love, things will eventually turn out right even though sometimes they may take longer than you want. So be patient with lessons of life for impatience often results in unnecessary mistakes and missed lessons.

To live a life filled with God's presence, you must make your actions be guided by God's love.

True action that yields true spiritual fruits should be done in alignment with God's dream for you. This means when you act, you are doing it for the love of God. When you go to work, you would do so to put God's hands to work. In effect you begin to work without working, for then it's God within you that's working through you.

The actions that flow from the fountain of love are imbued with love. So to love life is to love without conditions placed on those we extend our love to. It's in so loving that we build bridges of lasting friendships, friendships that can last an eternity.

An average person oftentimes performs actions for self–gain. One above average engages in actions that may be done to help another. It's a rare person whose actions are geared toward serving all life without expectation of anything in return.

Think of God in whatever you do. Make that your primary inspiration. And all your actions will yield nothing but growth toward God, for they are done to serve God.

To begin to know God, you must do two things: Learn the laws of God and apply them. Secondly, you must love your fellow man as you love yourself.

Spiritual laws are but governing forces that bring harmony and order to life so more Divine love can be manifested. With this love manifesting through you as a channel for Divine Spirit, you ought to do something with it—share it with others.

I n loving your fellow human being as you love
yourself, you are honoring their divinity.

Loving your fellow human being has many spiritual benefits that go beyond you and extend to making this world a better place as more love is allowed into this world. So learn to love unconditionally, so that pure love can manifest uninterruptedly for the upliftment of society. It's in fulfilling the law of love that you come into alignment with God.

Truth being what it is, it's never what we expect it to be. Oftentimes, it is different from what we expect. But the lover of truth is open to receiving the truth under all conditions and in all forms.

By connecting with others through loving actions do we serve God well.

I t's noteworthy that when love increases its outflow in a community, there's order that follows. The order follows because love has the power to make people behave with civility and more lovingly toward one another.

With love in your heart, you become connected to this life force in a way that gives you insight into how it operates. So look to cultivate Divine love in your heart, and you will be able to gain deeper understanding of life and its mysteries.

God knows you have served It by taking action to serve others unselfishly. So listen up, take action, and be grateful you served. You have had God's seeds of God's beauty and love planted in places more than you will ever know, for God's spirit may take those seeds further, beyond the initial point of distribution.

Love is the only gift from God, which when you sincerely partake of it, you become transformed to the extent that you are rendered more spiritual, awakened to life around you, and more love as it comes your way.

Divine love makes one ready and willing to go beyond limits of self-interest, self-indulgence, and self-centeredness. When this happens, a veil beyond where truth lies gets broken. From then on, you will no longer be the same. You will walk this earth a free person.

L ove is the only element in life here and beyond, which contains qualities that render anything it touches holy, golden, beautiful, uplifting, and above all, spiritual.

L ove has power in it, which, once understood, can raze to the ground anything negative that stands in its way.

Once you give love to where it finds a ready and open heart that receives it in fullness, life changes for you. Life becomes vibrant; life becomes enriched. You begin to feel a new energy surge permeate through your entire being. A feeling of openness, light heartedness, and well–being replaces the old feeling of constriction and heaviness. This is because the heart opens up to its greater capacity.

Where there's more love in the community, an increased sense of harmony permeates through the area. This is so because people become more in tune with the laws of nature and Divine Spirit, therefore, they walk in unison with life's rhythm.

When you love someone, love opens the other person's heart to receiving. This happens when the two Souls are aligned with each other—mentally, emotionally, and more importantly, spiritually. There's an uninterrupted flow of love that takes place. This flow is dynamic. It touches all aspects of the lives of individuals involved. Their lives become literally touched by the Golden light of God.

Spiritual truth lies in the inner God worlds. Absolute truth exists not in the lower worlds. You can live in the higher states while you maintain your physical presence here. In doing so, you will be living a higher life of spirit from whence inner strength, health, courage, wisdom, love, and spiritual freedom come.

CHAPTER 5
SOUL'S VIEW

By nature, Soul is joyful, therefore, even though It may experience loss in the physical world, which may yield temporary absence of joy in the human state, it's in this loss that It realizes the impermanency of mundane things.

If we get into the habit of opening ourselves to the voice of God, we will be keeping ourselves open to receiving God's guidance more readily.

A closed heart can never hear the voice of God. It can never embrace with great depth, the beauty, and joy that comes from God.

The purpose of Divine Spirit in this physical world and other planes of existence in which there still exist life in impure states, is to lift and bring purity to all that It touches.

The higher laws are there to make us live in this world but not of it. But more so of a higher spiritual world that is designed to guide and govern our higher actions.

Truth in its unadulterated pure state can only be revealed to an honest and loving heart.

Watch your dreams for they may provide insights and answers to many issues that may be at hand.

To look at life from a single point—human perspective only—is to engage in, unwittingly, untruths or partial truths that can lead one to false conclusions about who and what one is. In order to have a clear view of oneself, one must step out of the usual human consciousness and assume a different but higher viewpoint.

Who you are is a larger and harder question for many people to understand. You can't understand who you are at the human level because that entails going beyond the mind. This requires ascendance to higher consciousness.

If you are able to detach yourself from the mind and its influence, you will regain control of your life from the perspective of Soul. You will see life differently from a clear, lofty, and pure consciousness.

A loving heart is a truth detector. It sees truth where it exists; therefore, it sees love even though the outer illusory appearance may not immediately show it. A pure heart sees beyond the drama and the ostentatious display of wealth. It sees beyond the unbecoming façade of poverty.

How you view life may influence what choices you make, and consequently, what actions you take. View life from a position of impossibility, and life becomes impossible for you. View life from the position of limitless possibility, and maintain a can–do attitude, and a life of success becomes a possibility.

Try to view everything that seems difficult and challenging as a gift that God, via Divine Spirit, is bringing to you to help you work through, so you can move closer to your own self–discovery as Soul with limitless power and potential.

Practice listening to your heart more often. If you get into that habit, you will learn that there's a subtle, gentle inner voice of God that comes to guide you in what God wants you to do.

If we are able to view life from the perspective of Soul, we would live differently, conduct ourselves differently, view life differently, and treat others differently. It is in this heightened Soul perspective that we would gain greater view and insight into what's going on the surface–our outer life–so that where it may appear to be peaceful on the surface, there may lurk danger awaiting us. Whereas where it may seem chaotic on the surface, it may belie potential order and peace to soon ensue.

Never judge anything by its outer appearance. Always take time to look beyond the surface of any outer appearance for under there lays the truth and substance of it.

At the human level, you are limited with what you can see. Divine Spirit has infinite sight, therefore, It sees and knows what is good for you in all aspects of your life.

Always look to God for perfect guidance as to whom to give love and when best to do it.

Not everyone realizes that a lot of things that seem to go wrong do so, because we have in some way caused them by our stubbornness, negligence, greed, sense of self-righteousness, ignorance, laziness, or disdain for spiritual laws.

The food of God never fully quenches your desire for God. But it ignites it and causes you to want it more. If heaven can be experienced, even briefly, its wondrous beauty will leave you wanting more.

Be open and watchful as to how things play out in your life, and listen in for the hidden messages. Pay attention to the people you meet, what they say, the messages around your surroundings, and events as they happen. These are avenues Divine Spirit may use to pass on a message to you as It works to protect and guide you.

When in doubt, check with the inner voice of God. Once you get the inner message, go with it. It's always the first message that is accurate.

Loving life at a deeper level entails surrendering your personal self-interest into the hands of God. When this happens, you are inviting God to come through to be an integral part of your experience.

It takes an attitude of trust and being in a state of expectancy for higher truth to ready your heart to receive truth: an attitude of surrendering all life, all actions, all thoughts to God. In other words, one must have a loving attitude.

When you think outside the box, you are in actuality using your creative faculties to access ideas that are by nature outside the realm of common social, political, or any set structure that has been accepted as status quo.

For life to have a higher purpose and deeper meaning, you must give back in some constructive way to serve life. In so doing, you will not only be helping yourself move forward, you will be helping others experience love, joy, and beauty as you become a source from which they get inspired to live a better life.

Anything that brings you a step down, thus lowers your consciousness, is often from the mind in its base state. And that which brings you a step up is from God perceived through the heart center. So listen closely to your heart, so you can hear when God speaks.

Listen for God, but don't let the mind guide your listening approach. Listen more with your heart than your mind. Your heart is never biased in its reception and perception of God's guidance. So follow your heart, for you will be following God's voice.

Keep in mind that God's voice is present all the time, awaiting us to tune in to It. It's ourselves who are not present with It, therefore, we are not able to hear It. So to remain in tune with God's voice; we need to turn on our inner ears.

One way to keep your heart open is by finding out what you love to do and doing it. In doing it, your life will turn around for the better. So look to God to be shown what you need to do in the moment and with your life if you already don't know or you are in doubt.

What would God do if it were in your position with what you have? A question of this nature would shift your viewpoint from individual human self to a higher spiritual center that is a true permanent, most pure center of love in you. Acting from this vantage point, only good can come out of it.

Many people don't realize that the greatest of life fulfillment is ultimately found in life beyond this impermanent material world. It is found in the higher world whence beauty, freedom, love, and joy emanate.

Chant HU, the secret name for God, regularly, at a vocal level or mentally, depending on the situation. Learn to listen to God with your heart. When your heart is open by chanting HU, listen to God with an open heart. An open heart, by its inherent nature, can enable you to hear the voice of God, often in a nonverbal, telepathic way.

P eople who are creative in certain areas are so because they are engaged in an activity they love that opens them to their innermost part of themselves–the presence of God, which we all have.

If you consciously make God your true home, life will reflect that which you are a conscious part of.

God is the source of all that exists here and other worlds unknown to an ordinary man. When you recognize God's existence as an extension of all forms of life, you will begin to love all life. In doing so, you will begin to fall in love with God.

For more information about other books by the author and book orders.

Please visit:

Website: Ericchifundabooks.com

Twitter: EricChifunda@Chifundaeric

Lightning Source UK Ltd.
Milton Keynes UK
UKHW020632060820
367798UK00011B/1054

9 781951 775162